DATE DUE			

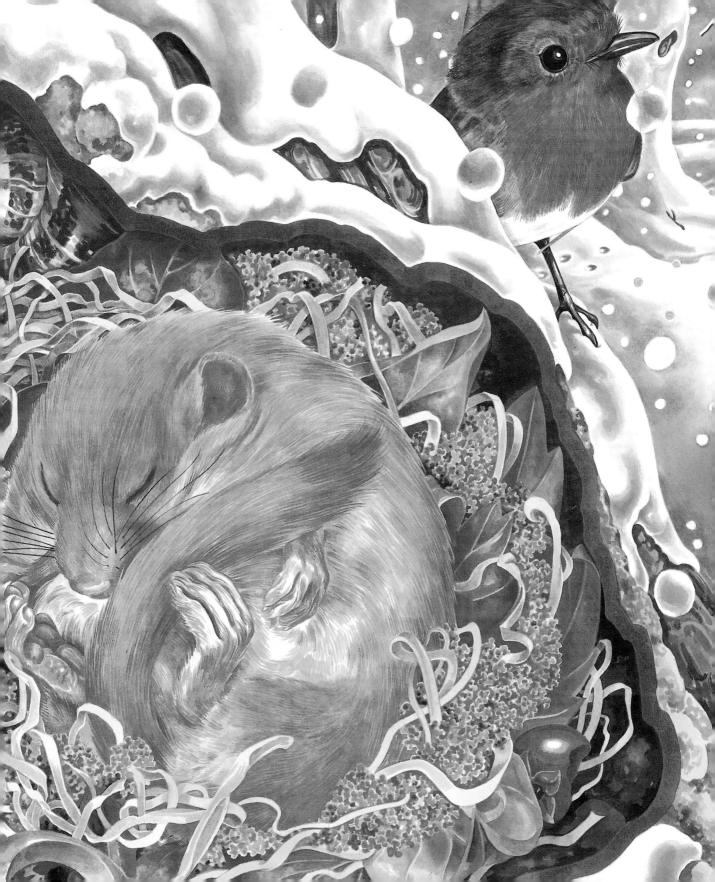

• CYCLES OF LIFE •
Hibernation

Written and illustrated by Carolyn Scrace
Created and designed by David Salariya

W
FRANKLIN WATTS
A Division of Scholastic Inc.
NEW YORK • TORONTO • LONDON • AUCKLAND • SYDNEY
MEXICO CITY • NEW DELHI • HONG KONG
DANBURY, CONNECTICUT

Contents

Introduction

When it is cold, animals cannot find much food. Some go to sleep for the whole **winter**. This is called hibernation.

In the months before they hibernate, the animals eat as much as possible to get fat. During hibernation, their bodies use up this fat. They get very cold and thin. Their breathing and heartbeat also slow down.

In the warm **spring** weather, the hibernating animals wake up again.

Bears, bats, squirrels, and dormice are all animals that hibernate.

Fox

Squirrel

Rabbits

Finding Food

In the early **autumn**, the dormouse can find plenty of food.

It eats nuts, seeds, fruit, **bark**, and **shoots**. It also eats **snails** and **insects**.

Hawthorn berries

Snail

Hazelnut

Leaves ———————

Digging a Hole

Later in the autumn
there is less food for the
dormouse to eat.

It starts digging a hole
under leaves or the roots
of a tree.

In the autumn, the
days get shorter and
the weather gets colder.
Leaves start to fall off
the trees, and many
plants die.

Eating Hazelnuts

The dormouse likes the taste of **hazelnuts**.

First it gnaws a hole in the shell with its strong lower teeth. Then it eats the **kernel** inside.

The dormouse eats so many hazelnuts that it becomes very fat.

Blackberry

Snail

Earthworm

The snail is also
looking for shelter
from the cold.

Ready to
Build a Nest

The dormouse
has finished
digging its hole.

The hole is just
the right size for
a **nest**.

15

The magpie has found a juicy worm to eat.

Magpie

Making the Nest Comfortable

The dormouse uses **moss**, leaves, and grass to make its nest warm and comfortable.

It will spend five months hibernating inside the nest.

Hiding the Entrance

The nest is now finished.

The dormouse hides the entrance to the nest with soil and leaves.

19

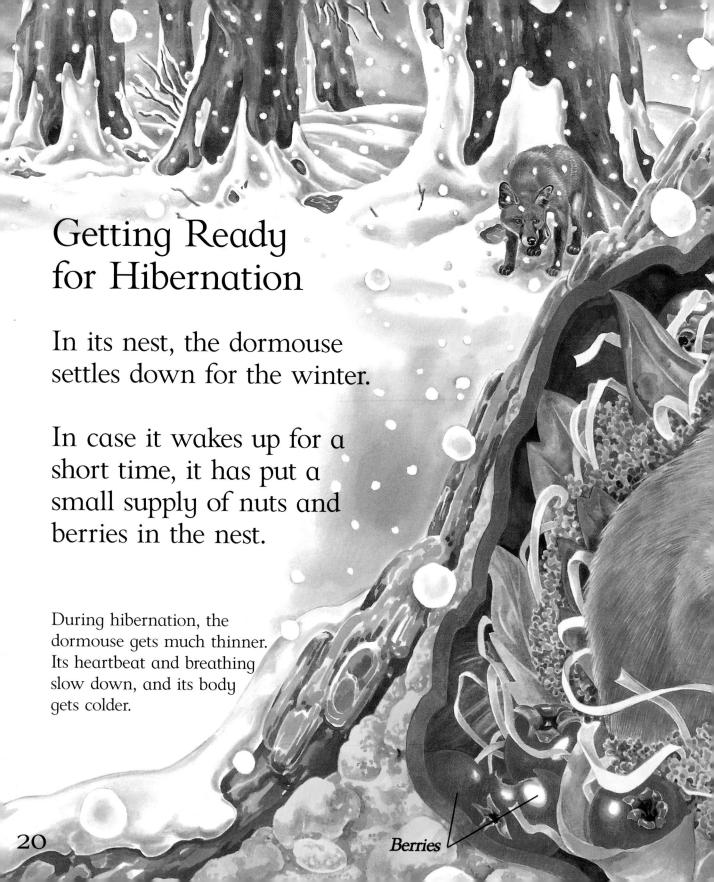

Getting Ready
for Hibernation

In its nest, the dormouse
settles down for the winter.

In case it wakes up for a
short time, it has put a
small supply of nuts and
berries in the nest.

During hibernation, the
dormouse gets much thinner.
Its heartbeat and breathing
slow down, and its body
gets colder.

Berries

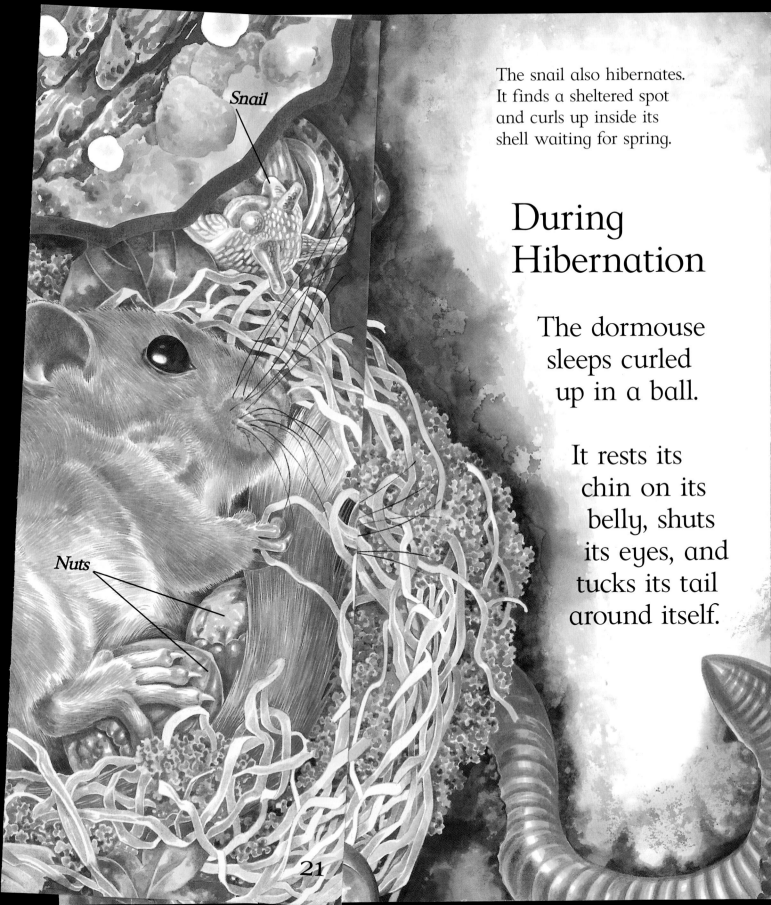

Snail

Nuts

The snail also hibernates. It finds a sheltered spot and curls up inside its shell waiting for spring.

During Hibernation

The dormouse sleeps curled up in a ball.

It rests its chin on its belly, shuts its eyes, and tucks its tail around itself.

21

In the spring, the trees grow new leaves and shoots. Spring flowers begin to grow.

Magpies

Rabbits

Bluebells

Waking Up

In the spring, the weather gets warmer. The dormouse wakes up.

It takes the little animal twelve hours to wake up from its hibernation.

As the earth warms up,
the snail also wakes up
and comes out of its shell.

Leaving the Nest

The dormouse has
survived the long,
cold winter months.

It is now very
hungry. It
climbs out of its
nest and goes
in search of
food again.

27

The Dormouse's Year

During the summer and early autumn, the dormouse eats lots of food.

In late autumn, the dormouse picks a safe place to dig a hole for its nest.

The dormouse uses bits of grass, leaves, and moss to build its nest.

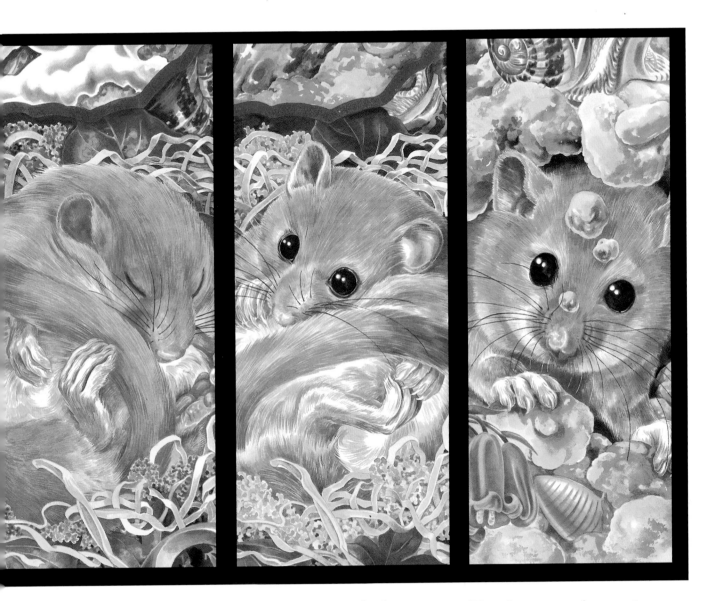

From late autumn until the middle of spring, the dormouse hibernates.

Five to six months later, in the middle of spring, the dormouse wakes up.

The dormouse leaves its nest and goes in search of food. It starts to eat again.

Hibernation Words

Autumn
The months of September, October, and November, when the weather gets cold

Bark
The tough outer covering of a tree

Hazelnut
The small fruit or nut of the hazel tree

Insect
An animal that has a hard outer covering and a body divided into three parts: the head, the thorax, and the abdomen. Insects have six legs.

Kernel
The part of a nut that can be eaten, found inside the hard shell

Moss
A small green plant that grows on damp soil and some trees and rocks

Nest
A bed or shelter made by an animal

Shoots
The new, young growth on plants and trees

Snail
An animal that does not have any bones. It has a hard spiraled shell and a soft body.

Spring
The months of March, April, and May, when the weather begins to get warmer

Winter
The months of December, January, and February, when the weather is very cold

Index

31

Created, designed and produced by
The Salariya Book Company Ltd
Book House,
25 Marlborough Place,
Brighton BN1 1UB

First published in 2002 by Franklin Watts
A Division of Scholastic Inc.

A catalog record for this title is available from the
Library of Congress.

ISBN 0-531-14657-X (Lib. Bdg.)
ISBN 0-531-14842-4 (Pbk.)

Printed and bound in China.

Franklin Watts
90 Sherman Turnpike
Danbury, CT 06816

Natural History Consultant   Dr. Gerald Legg
Language Consultant   Betty Root

Editor   Karen Barker Smith
Assistant Editor   Stephanie Cole